Change the Conversation

Teens, Dating & The Church

by Samantha Hanni with Kurtis Hanni

CHANGE THE CONVERSATION

Printed by CreateSpace

ISBN-13: 978-1533408686

ISBN-10: 1533408688

All Scripture quotations, unless otherwise indicated, are taken from The Holy Bible, New International Version RR, NIV RR, Copyright CC 1973, 1978, 1984, 2011 by Biblica, Inc. TM Used by permission. All right reserved worldwide.

Scripture quotations from The Authorized (King James) Version. Rights in the Authorized Version in the United Kingdom are vested in the Crown. Reproduced by permission of the Crown's patentee, Cambridge University Press

All rights reserved. No part of this publication may be reproduced, stored in a retrieval system, or transmitted in any form or by any means—electronic, mechanical, photocopy, recording, or any other—expect for brief quotations in printed reviews, without the prior permission of the publisher.

For my love, KWH.

For Claire, because this
book wouldn't have
happened without you!

Table of Contents

Intro: Can We Stop Talking About Dating? 1

Part One

    Chapter One: What Are You Building On? 11

    Chapter Two: What is Purity? 25

Part Two

    Chapter Three: Change Your Intentions 37

    Chapter Four: Change Your Expectations 51

    Chapter Five: Change the Atmosphere 65

Part Three

    Chapter Six: In the Meantime: For Ladies 83

    Chapter Seven: In the Meantime: For Guys 93

Afterword: Yeah, But Waiting Still Sucks 109

Conclusion: After the Honeymoon 113

INTRODUCTION

Can We Stop Talking About Dating?

Dating. For a word the Bible never uses, Christians have ridden it hard, and this generation happens upon it like mounting a worn-out race horse, unfit to run its course.

Whether in books, seminars, sermons, or songs, the trappings and connotations of Christian dating are tired, empty, and ineffective. I know what you're probably thinking: *Seriously, another dating book? What else is there to say?*

A lot needs to be said, actually, so hang in here with me.

In my own life, and through years of teaching youth in different capacities, I've seen firsthand how the church has failed to hold meaningful, ongoing conversations with its youth and young adults on what dating is and should be. It's failed to paint purity as a lifestyle; a lifestyle to be pursued before and during marriage, not a checklist of do's and don'ts. Teens are less equipped to recognize unrealistic expectations in their dating relationships and consequently less able to recalibrate those expectations. It's minimized the importance of *being* the right person, and maximized the hunt *for* the right person. Or at the least, it hasn't said anything to the contrary.

This stunted communication forces Christian teens and young adults to find answers elsewhere, or else harbor a lot of unanswered questions and trudge through a forest of guilt, confusion, unrealistic expectations, and poor communication. Questions like *What does purity actually look like in real life? What's wrong with me that all my friends are dating/engaged/married but me? I've been told to stay away from sex my whole life, and now that I'm married, it's supposed to be good? How do I process that? Why did my parents never talk about this? What is my role in the relationship? Am I being too forward? Not open enough? How often can I initiate conversations through calls and texts? How much is too much? How little is too little?*

Any of those questions sound familiar?

I realized my dating principles only took me so far when I put them into practice in my first dating relationship. All of a sudden, I felt like I was holding the Cliff Notes version to dating, rather than the full text of what was supposed to be done, said, and avoided. All that I had read, prayed about, and talked about since I was in middle school, all the notions I had about dating were good ideas, right ideas even, but I found them...lacking.

Those Notions and Ideas

A lot of my notions and ideas about dating came from a source many Christian young adults will be familiar with. The List.

You know, *The List.* That list that almost all Christian teens start in middle school and keep until their engagement: the list of qualities desired in a spouse. The list usually starts after a particular lesson in Sunday school or youth group, and girls eagerly record what they consider as husband material: tall, plays guitar, loves Jesus, or something like that. Boys start to consider that there's more to be desired than a girl who just laughs at every joke or has a hot body.

But there it is, expectations are voiced and recorded for posterity sake in prayer journals across the nation. Maybe after a few years, the vibrant hopefulness of the list dims, but it's still there in the back of every youth group kid's mind. I know it was for me.

After different friendships throughout college, and my first dating relationship, I felt my own list was in need of revision. Words look a lot different in person than they do on paper, a fact which is hard to perceive in eighth grade. The summer before my senior year in college, and on the cusp of beginning my relationship with my future husband, this is where I found myself: "backspacing" notions and ideas I had held for a long time and squaring up with reality. Future relationships looked nice and tidy on paper. They always do. But in reality, relationships are messy and evolving.

While goals help define the direction you're heading, a list mentality can harbor unrealistic expectations. I spent some time revising my list, whittling it down to just nine items. Nine. The list in its original form held over twenty items.

Not even a month after this revision, a mutual friend set Kurtis and I up on a blind date (through a series of crazy events), and we agreed to meet for coffee one evening. We hit it off that night, went on a real date a few days later, and became an official couple about a month after meeting for the first time. I was 21 and Kurtis was 25 when we met. He had already graduated college, started a second job, and owned a house and a car. I was in my last year in college, and while not fully established on my own, I was in a more mature and stable place than say, at 16. We had both had previous relationships, and for where we were in life, dating in its current form seemed cumbersome and juvenile. We both had marriage as the ultimate goal in a dating relationship. How do we intentionally pursue God with this new relationship? How do we make the most of our time? These were just some of the questions we asked ourselves as we began to get to know each other, and it set the tone for our dating relationship and eventually our marriage.

This is our story, our experiences. You maybe have had vastly differently experiences. Maybe you'll catch glimpses of yourself in our pages. Whatever may be the case, my goal in sharing a slice of our life is that you'll have the courage to change the conversation about dating. You may be feeling frustrated or disillusioned with your dating journey, wondering if this is all there is. You may be wanting a fresh perspective to voice your thoughts. My hope is that you'll find a nugget of truth that encourages you like so many other conversations encouraged me throughout my high school and college years. I pray you also catch the vision that there's a better path to follow with our approach to dating and relationships. It's about being intentional. We did it, and we promise if you approach dating in this way, you'll experience the benefits of well-spent time, healthy relationships and a deeper trust in God. Our story is not a formula. There is no hidden method out there that you just haven't discovered yet. But there are key elements present in any successful relationship. Our experience supports this. Outside research concurs. And above all, God's word confirms it.

Sound good? On board? Let's start talking. Let's change the conversation.

PART ONE

CHAPTER ONE

What Are You Building On?

Every house, office building, or skyscraper starts with a foundation. A strong, level, smooth foundation. If it doesn't start on a level foundation; well, things can get messy. A slight fault in any foundation can throw off measurements for the walls. If the measurements are off, adjustments must be made elsewhere, ultimately weakening the whole structure.

Have you ever realized that your heart is like an amazing skyscraper under construction? What are you building on? Are you building on God's love, or something else that is faulty? God's love doesn't "crack" or change. His love won't fail us, for he is a trustworthy foundation. Sure, there will be imperfections along the way since we are human and live in a fallen world. But those imperfections won't interfere with the the integrity of the foundation.

As children of God, a relationship with Jesus is that foundation for all other relationships. God's love is a strong, level foundation on which your entire life is built, including any relationships, romantic or otherwise.

Although other lessons took (and still take) me longer to learn, I took this one to heart during middle school and high school. Jesus gave me such a vibrant image of his love filling my heart, laying that foundation before any man came along. I was irresistibly drawn to this truth. In this crucial time of developing spiritually and emotionally, I learned to let God define who I was.

"For you created my inmost being;
you knit me together in my mother's
womb. I praise you because I am

> *fearfully and wonderfully made;*
> *your works are wonderful, I know*
> *that full well."* Psalm 139:13-14 (NIV)

When I did begin to build more friendships with guys and start dating as I got older, a firm foundation was in place. I had solid ground to stand on as I interacted with new friends, knowing that my worth couldn't be taken away, my purpose couldn't be hijacked, and at the end of the day, God always delighted in me and would never fail me. I want to be sure you heard me: God assigns your worth, and you are more valuable to him than any precious stone. Who doesn't want to be assured of worth, purpose, and a God who will never fail us?

Too often though, we stray from our foundation and look to satisfy these desires in other pursuits, possessions, or relationships. God created us with all these desires: a desire for purpose, a desire for meaning, and a desire to be delighted in and loved. He created us with those desires, and then he himself is the perfect answer to those desires. The Bible shows time and again that he assigns our worth, he gives us purpose, he delights in us, and he never fails us. No human can deliver perfectly on those promises, so we need to stop expecting others to do what only God can do.

He Assigns Our Worth

It was my 21st birthday. I walked my first boyfriend out the door and gave him a hug, and he gave me a peck on my temple. Seems innocent enough, right? Later I texted him, "Thank you for that sweet birthday kiss." He replied with something I should've seen coming.

"A real kiss next time?"

My heart fluttered, but not in a good way.

While I couldn't articulate it at the time, this young man didn't appear to live *intentionally,* and it stunted the growth of our relationship. Sure, he was sweet to me, charming, and had a good relationship with his family. But he also lived at home with no concrete plan for changing that situation, he wasn't diligently pursuing a higher education, and he didn't attend church on his own. Our relationship already had some red flags, and to me a kiss, *the kiss*, was a big deal. I wasn't sure he would be the man I would marry. While I didn't believe I needed to save my first kiss for my wedding day, my first kiss did signify giving away a special part of my heart. I didn't trust this guy with that honor.

I told him no, and he didn't like that. For the next several days, our communication was strained, and the first time I tried to meet face-to-face, he said he couldn't because he was going out for drinks that night with another friend...who was a girl. We broke up two days later.

Why do I share this story? I want you to see that your worth is not defined by a significant other who wants to kiss, wants to hold hands, or anything of that nature. If that were the case, much of life might feel worthless. As children of God, is that how we are supposed to live our lives? Feeling worthless? I think not.

A common event in action-packed movies or maybe even our own fantasies is someone rushing in to save a victim (or us) from a burning building or a burning car. We revel in the fact that someone thinks we would be worth saving. We marvel at someone who would be willing to risk their own life because they thought we were worth it. Guess what? That's already happened. (Hint: the cross, Jesus, tomb) Someone did think you were worth saving. God sacrificed His only Son for us, and in doing so, he saved you from a fiery eternal home.

> "For God so loved the world that he gave his one and only Son, that whoever believes in him shall not perish but have eternal life." John 3:16 (NIV)

Your maker, your savior, has already assigned you great worth. You don't have to search for it elsewhere. I could've given into my first boyfriend's desire for a kiss on the lips to meet my desire to be liked, to be a "good" girlfriend. No, the world wouldn't have ended, but who knows where that would've led? Who knows what I would've given up next?

He Gives Us Purpose

What is your purpose in life? If you had to give the famous "elevator pitch" about your life, how would you condense it into a two-minute spiel? Is it to be an entrepreneur? Is it to get married? Is it to write books? Is it to play professional sports? Is it to be in ministry?

As Christians, no matter what our vocation, our main purpose is to know and follow Christ, and tell others about Him. It's that simple. It starts and ends with Christ. If our purpose starts and ends with ourselves, or starts and ends with someone else, we've missed the point. It's like inserting the plug of a power strip in the strip itself, instead of the wall. There's no power, no energy. There's no lasting power in amassing a fortune, accumulating accolades, or becoming "the best" in whatever field because ultimately, those things fade away. There's no joy in trying to hold on to people that constantly desert you. These things don't last. They don't satisfy in the quiet moments when no one else is around. We have to plug into God to understand our full purpose.

> "Guard the good deposit that was entrusted to you—guard it with the help of the Holy Spirit who lives in us." 2 Timothy 1:14 (NIV)

God has blessed each of His kids with passions and gifts that he wants to be explored and developed for use in the kingdom of God. He wants to build a relationship with us. He wants us to fill the earth with the knowledge of him. For many of us, our journey here on earth does include meeting someone we can build our life with. But that is a part of the journey, not the journey itself.

He Delights in Us

You know what it's like. That guy or girl you've been "talking to" eventually stops talking. A few less texts per day. Less enthusiasm. Shorter responses. Soon the texts slow to a trickle and then they stop.

What happened? Did you suddenly become boring and repulsive? Was it something you said? Was it something you didn't say? Around and around our brains spin trying to figure out what broke down in between two innocent cell phones and one promising friendship.

This has happened to all of us at one point or another, and it's hurtful every time. Sometimes it's more hurtful than actual breakups, because we don't know what happened. It's easy to think that something is inherently wrong with us, and that after a while, others will get bored with us, or get intimidated and fade into the shadows.

I still struggle with these fears today and at times, project them onto my husband and even my relationship with God. I'm afraid that those closest to me will get tired of me and just...leave.

"Since you are precious and honored in my sight and because I love you..."
Isaiah 43:4 (NIV)
The Lord your God is with you, the Mighty Warrior who saves. He will take great delight in you; in his love he will no longer rebuke you, but will rejoice over you with singing."
Zephaniah 3:17 (NIV)

The Lord takes great delight in you. He's not going to get tired of you, quit talking to you, or grow bored of your hang-ups and complaints. When he uses words like "precious," "great delight," "rejoice," and "love," that sounds like someone who is committed to his bride.

It's true that people will fade into the background of our lives. Sometimes the Lord allows people to cross our paths, and then keep walking. It hurts. It's confusing. But it doesn't have to derail us. If we are secure in the fact that God takes great delight in us, we can be free to learn all we can from the friendships in our lives, and let go when it's time.

He Never Fails Us

People are not perfect. They will fail you. Your significant other will fail you. Your best friend will fail you. Your parents will fail you. Your grandparents will fail you. Hopefully not all at the same time, but it's going to happen.

And guess what? You will fail others as well, because you too are human.

The gut-level grief when mistakes and errors are uncovered in a relationship is horrible. But we set ourselves up for greater disappointment when we place super-hero expectations on our significant other, when the only one who can support those expectations is God. He will never fail us.

"Be content with what you have, because God has said, 'Never

will I leave you; never will I forsake you.'" Hebrews 13:5 (NIV)

If you find yourself constantly frustrated and anxious in a relationship, ask yourself *what are my expectations of this other person?* Spend some time in thought and prayer, and honestly evaluate if these expectations are reasonable. Are you asking for constant affirmation and attention? Do you place unrealistic expectations on their time? Have both you and your significant other neglected friends and family to pour into this relationship? These are just some warning flags that one or both of you have placed unrealistic expectations on each other. The appropriate response is to recalibrate your expectations and set your focus on God. Next, have a conversation with that other person and acknowledge where you've been unreasonable. The relationship may be tuned up and ready to move forward, or it may be time to part ways. Either way, I pray you have the courage to keep Jesus as the foundation, and to not compromise.

Sharing Our Story

I don't often get to share this part of my story, but what most people don't realize is that this part was crucial to where I was spiritually and emotionally when Kurtis and I crossed paths. A month and a half before I met Kurtis, my grandpa committed suicide. His death was the final installment in a series of trials my family had endured the previous few months. Hurt, confusion, and grief scorched me during that horrible summer, and my heart felt like the withered grass that was in everyone's yard: parched and desperate for relief.

I remember more than one night in July laying in my bed and as cliché as it sounds, crying myself to sleep. I wrote letters to my grandpa, read his favorite passages from his favorite books, and missed him. I missed him so much. But God didn't leave me there. Because I had been faithfully building on the foundation, and diligently cultivating my relationship with the Lord, these trials burned away trivial complaints and hang-ups in my mind that didn't matter, and left me with what was truly necessary: God himself.

In those summer months, I was in His word and seeking comfort and peace like never before, and he comforted. I was asking for guidance and wisdom as I headed into my final year of college, and he guided. God faithfully delivered on His promises to me, strengthening my foundation even further. And he was about to deliver on yet another promise...

The Prayer

During this summer, one of the things I was praying about was my future husband. At the time, there was no one on my radar, and it seemed reasonable to ask that God let me at least meet the man I would marry sometime during my senior year.

The least God can say is no, right?

I had prayed for and about my husband for many years (remember I had my list), but this time felt different. I wrote out my request and placed it somewhere I could see it daily. One month after this prayer, I met Kurtis for the first time.

God doesn't work with formulas, so please don't look at my story and think that after one prayer, God will immediately answer. He had been moving and working behind the scenes unbeknownst to me, and it was just time. (He is working behind the scenes in your life too. Don't doubt it for one minute.) But I truly believe because I was in such a humble, trusting place in my relationship with Christ that I was ready to receive what God had for me.

Each day with God is preparing you for what's around the corner, so don't discount the small things. Don't diminish the details. We never know what's around the corner. It could be a death in the family. It could be a job opportunity or a scholarship. It could be meeting your spouse. Whatever the case may be, sink your roots deep in to God and rest in the fact that your worth is secure in him.

"Lord, you alone are my portion and my cup; you make my lot secure"
Psalm 16: 5 (NIV)

CHAPTER TWO

What is Purity?

> *"For he chose us in him before the creation of the world to be holy and blameless in his sight."* Ephesians 1:4 (NIV)

When you hear the word purity, what comes to mind? Is something pure by what is or isn't in it? Clean, white sheets free of stains? Cold, clear water with no dirt or grime? A product free of harsh chemicals or additives? Merriam-Webster defines purity as the following:

> *Pure: 1: unmixed with any other matter; free from dust, dirt, or taint; spotless, stainless. 2: being thus and no other. 3: free from what vitiates, weakens, or pollutes; containing nothing that does not properly belong; free from moral fault or guilt; marked by chastity.1*

There is no shortage of dialogue on the concept of purity in Christian circles. No talking to other people while the dating relationship is still young? No hand-holding until engagement? Hand-holding with no kissing? Kissing, but no touching? Anything short of intercourse? I've heard some use the measuring stick of anything you do with your dad, you can do with your boyfriend: a peck on the cheek, handholding, sitting next to each other on the couch. Many ideas. But which one is right? Is there a "right" one? Unlike a dictionary, there's no hard and fast definition of what constitutes purity in a dating relationship. Life would be much easier if that were the case. Or would it?

---

[1] http://www.merriam-webster.com/dictionary/pure

A Lifestyle, Not a List

This is one of the first topics where the conversation on Christian dating needs to change. Purity in light of the cross is not a checklist. You can't hold up a list and say "I haven't done any of these, so I must be pure," if your *heart* is not in the right place. Purity begins in your heart, with Jesus making your heart clean and whole. The journey of walking with the Lord is about learning what does and doesn't lead you closer to Christ, what fosters purity in your heart. So that would include your dating relationship, engagement, and more importantly, your marriage. Purity doesn't begin with a purity ring, and doesn't stop with a wedding ring. As Christians, purity is about how we live our lives, not some assignment to receive a grade on. Too often, the youth group talks and Sunday School lessons on purity in dating seem just like that: an assignment, a one-time pass or fail. A checklist to complete or not, and if you've already failed, what's the point in trying to make it right? Ever felt this way? You are not alone.

In a 2011 Barna study, meeting the church's expectations of sexual purity was cited as a big tension point for millennials in their faith, and came in at a number four on the list of why they were leaving the church.[2] Um, yikes.

There is no grace in a checklist. Jesus came to abolish checklist mentalities, because the Old Testament demonstrated that lists and laws can't change hearts on their own. They limit relationships. They emphasize works, not grace.

> *"For sin shall no longer be your master, because you are not under the law, but under grace." Romans 6:14 (NIV)*

Jesus came to change our hearts. He came so he could have a relationship with us. He came to save us from our works by his grace.

> *"And if by grace, then it cannot be based on works; if it were, grace*

---

[2] https://www.barna.org/barna-update/millennials/528-six-reasons-young-christians-leave-church

would no longer be grace." Romans 11:6 (NIV)

Sheila Wray Gregoire is a Christian author and blogger. I love this statement in one of her posts on purity:

> *"We don't stay pure until we're married. We stay pure. Period. I'm married and I'm pure. And yet the way that we phrase it makes it sound as if you lose your purity the moment you have sex—even if sex is with your husband."*[3]

A part of the parents' job in discipling their kids is to cast this vision of purity, a vision that inspires them to actually reach the goal, and pass it on to their kids. The vision should be a lifelong pursuit of the things that honor God and bring them closer to him. Yes, there is a need for expectations and boundaries, but they can't be the goal themselves. Rigid rules that focus *only* on behavior control fall

---

[3] http://tolovehonorandvacuum.com/2016/01/purity-culture-10-things-that-scare-me

short of where the problem lies: in the heart. Instead, it only serves to create more friction and more motivation for rebellion.

However, if you're in a dating relationship and if you are *only* looking for a checklist, then it sounds like you have already planned in your heart to get as close as you can to the fire without getting burned. That isn't pursuing purity either.

In Proverbs 6, we find the author warning his son against the trap of illegitimate relationships.

> *"Can a man scoop fire into his lap without his clothes being burned? Can a man walk on hot coals without his feet being scorched?" vs. 27-28 (NIV)*

These verses always come to mind when pondering the question "how far is too far?" We've all asked it, either out loud or in our hearts. But the truth is, if you walk too close to the line, eventually you'll find yourself venturing on the other side.

What is the better question then? Rather than pursuing what makes you feel good without doing "it," ask yourself instead if your thoughts, words, and actions are leading you closer to who God wants you to be.

Embrace the Awkwardness

Some of you might be thinking at this point that I'm against all boundaries in dating relationships. Not true. They need to be there for the same reason we wear seat belts in the car, or stay inside the guardrails on a highway. They aren't there to take away our fun, but give us greater freedom by keeping us safe. Boundaries do serve a purpose, but they should be the vehicle for the goal you are pursuing, not the goal itself. Boundaries aren't there to separate you from the fun, but to define the path before you. They are a means to an end, not the end itself.

Yes, talking about boundaries with your significant other is one of the most delicate and awkward conversations you can have. So is having that discussion with your parents on what they desire while you live under their roof. I'm not denying this fact. However, I learned to not be so afraid to talk about boundaries early, and to not be afraid to revisit the topic. It is normal and necessary to return to this conversation as the relationship develops, and to make sure both of you have your hearts in the right place. It will be awkward, but part of growing up and having adult relationships is learning how to have those awkward conversations. Even in marriage, there are still awkward conversations to be had. So don't use that as an excuse.

Also, decisions on boundaries can't be made in the heat of the moment. Make those decisions when there are as a few emotions attached to the moment as possible. That's why early on in the relationship can be a good time to have that talk, as you two may not be as emotionally involved yet.

Pursuing purity in dating relationships is hard. But that doesn't mean it shouldn't be your goal. Spoiler: you will make mistakes. You just will, because you are human. We do our best to walk closely with the Lord, and when we do make mistakes, confess. Most people don't look back at their dating relationships and think *Gosh, I wish I had pursued the physical side more. I wish I had kissed more. I wish we had felt each other up more.* No. If anything, you look back and wish you did *less*. So if you're afraid you're going to miss out on something before marriage, I would encourage you to think twice.

Kurtis and I did not do everything perfectly right. While we didn't sleep together, take clothes off, or lay in the same bed before marriage, we did linger longer than we should have with goodbyes that should've been a few kisses shorter. Physical contact can have a role, but it's not in the driver's seat for a Christian dating relationship. God has to be in the driver's seat from the beginning. My parents also laid down the rule that we couldn't spend dates alone at his house, or be alone in any house, but they opened their house frequently for us to hang out altogether. Kurtis' parents did the same.

We struggled with this rule and I had a bad attitude at times as a result. It was messier than I expected. My relationship with God was affected because of my stubborn desires, and it took a couple of years for me to even see the damage I had done to myself. But we did our best to keep our eyes on Jesus, and that's all we can do each and every day.

"Therefore, I urge you, brothers and sisters, in view of God's mercy, to offer your bodies as a living sacrifice, holy and pleasing to God—this is your true and proper worship. Do not conform to the pattern of this world, but be transformed by the renewing of your mind. Then you will be able to test and approve what God's will is—his good, pleasing and perfect will."
Romans 12:1-2 (NIV)

PART TWO

CHAPTER THREE

Change Your Intentions

Think about that feeling when your crush finally looks your way, or you hear from a friend of a friend that they actually like you. Or maybe think about the feeling when they finally sit next to you at lunch, or lo and behold when they finally give you their number, or ask for yours. Pretty great, right? Then what?

Should you just go for it? Wait for them to make the first move? If you're in college or beyond, it's easier to move forward with a new relationship. But what about if you are in high school? Dating in high school can be very limited. There are limitations on where you live, where you go, and how you get there. Financial resources are limited.

Again, there are a lot of schools of thought on when the appropriate age to start dating should be. And again, I don't think there is one right answer. I'm not here to tell you if dating in middle school/high school is a good or bad thing. There are plenty of other books written that take one side or the other. What I am offering is a different way to look at any dating relationship.

Why should you even care? I'm glad you asked.

People matter. You matter. Your friends matter. People's hearts and minds are precious things to be handled with care in God's view. During your school years, it's a prime opportunity to practice building friendships and learn to live in community with other believers.

What isn't valuable, and what won't help you grow one bit, is to hyper-focus on your love life. Since transportation, money, jobs, and other resources are limited in high school, is it really the best use of your time to be pursuing a series of relationships...just because? Because it's the popular thing? Because your friends think you and so-and-so would be just perfect together? Probably not. Perhaps you spend time just going on dates, but not committing to a relationship. That can work too, as it still allows you to get to know someone you feel merits more of your attention, but less pressure. No matter what age you are, you have the opportunity to change the conversation and approach these relationships with intention.

> *"So I do not run aimlessly; I do not box as one beating the air."*
> *1 Corinthians 9:26 (NIV)*

To arrive at any destination, you have to know where you are currently and where you are headed. That's what being intentional is all about. Be clear and reasonable about the stage of life you are in, and be clear about where you are headed. Be intentional about who you spend time with. Be intentional with your activities and conversations. Because if you don't, more than likely you will end up in a place you never planned on being.

For Kurtis and I, intentional choices became the theme of our dating relationship. We weren't just dating to have a good time; we were seriously evaluating each other to see if we were fit for life together. It was theme of our dating season, and we strive today to make it the theme of our marriage. Great things, like healthy, fun relationships don't just happen.

So how do you date intentionally? There are three areas that are important to be intentional about: your time, your choices, and your conversation. I would encourage you to pay close attention to these areas as your relationship develops, or as you develop habits before you start dating.

Time

From my observations in working with youth in a variety of circumstances, I still believe high school should be a time to focus on education, practice building friendships with girls and boys, and be less focused on romantic relationships. It's not to say relationships formed in high school can't last; that's more of an exception than the rule however. In high school and even into your first year out of high school, you are still becoming *you*. To become too quickly and too deeply attached to another person at this stage isn't always a good thing.

Looking back at where I was my senior year in high school to my freshman year in college, I changed so much. I grew more emotionally and spiritually in that freshman year than all the years before. New school routine, leadership expectations with my scholarship, and tons of new friends challenged me almost daily. I was glad I didn't have a relationship to juggle at the same time.

Too often, dating relationships become the priority for teens. They become the driving force behind how you think, act, dress, and move in your social circles. A young relationship can quickly become ill-balanced. A bad balance of priorities in relationships shows up in monopolizing of time, jealousy when one person hangs out with another group of people, and excessive controlling words. This puts a limp in young relationships, and can set a pattern for future relationships in your life. So whether you choose to date in high school, or choose to wait, guard your time during this season. Make your intentions clear for yourself and for others.

Choices

There are positives to young dating. I won't say they don't exist. Dating young means you have a chance to create deeper relationships with the opposite sex. These relationships can lead to more functional dating relationships in the future. When you get older and date "for real," you have less kinks to work out. Young dating can help shape who you are, increase your confidence, and help you grow into the person you should be.

While I chose to not date in high school, Kurtis did. Young dating took him from an insecure and unconfident teenager to a point where he had confidence. This confidence made him more willing to open up, helped him overcome my shyness, and helped shape his personality. It was a choice that was beneficial to him.

Once we met and began dating, our choices and activities were also intentional. Yes, we had "fun." But in the short time that we dated before we got engaged (only eight months!) we also spent time getting to know each other's families, seeking out entertainment that led us closer to the Lord, and began developing our spiritual lives together. We spent a lot of time over at my parents' house, and his parents' house, including their wisdom and their friendship in our budding relationship. We chose movies and other dates that led us closer to the Lord, not farther away.

Once we were engaged, we began to pray and seek God together more and more. We went to church together, prayed for each other, read different books on marriage together. But I add a caution to this: this can make the boundaries tougher to keep! Something about that Holy Spirit moving when your significant other prays for you...it's powerful is all I can say.

Another choice we made was waiting a long time to have any physical contact other than hugs. We did discuss boundaries a few days after our first date, but didn't circle back to it for several more months. Kurtis took extra care to not initiate physical contact during the first few months, and so I can genuinely say that we fell in love before we kissed. We didn't fall in love because we kissed. We didn't fall in love because of each other's bodies. I fell in love because of who he was. He fell in love because of who I was. I fell in love with his personality and quirks. I fell in love with his passions, goals, and desires. I fell in love with how he treated me. But more importantly, I fell in love with his heart for God.

Conversations

For Kurtis and I, there was a clear focus on marriage in regard to our conversations from the outset of the relationship. We of course had silly conversations, did crazy stuff (crazy by our standards), had disagreements and all of that normal stuff. But we also didn't shy away from hardcore topics: career goals, desire for kids, roles in marriage, money, family and personal issues. We talked about tithing, serving in the church, adoption, and education. We each shared our testimonies, and shared the times our faith went through incredible testing. Some things were easier to talk about than others, but the point is we talked about it. We spent the time delving into the topics that would shape our future together.

I remember going through our premarital counseling, and the pastor asking us many of the same things we had already covered between ourselves. The pastor said we would be surprised at how many couples don't talk about such things. What were they talking about if they weren't covering these topics? Digging into these areas gives the roots for your relationship room to grow. A shallow hole doesn't give roots the nutrition and space it needs to nourish the plant above. So dig deep, and in doing so, you will nourish that relationship.

If you don't know how you would answer those questions, and you are in a serious relationship, now is the time to get some answers.

The Power of Prayer

> *"Rejoice always, pray continually, give thanks in all circumstances; for this is God's will for you in Christ Jesus."*
> *1 Thessalonians 5:16-18 (NIV)*

The dating stage is also the perfect time to pray for who you will marry, and pray for the future family you will marry into. I cannot emphasize this enough.

Here are just a few things you can pray for you and your future spouse, because as much as you are hoping to meet the right person, you, my friend, ARE the right person for someone else. This is the time to grow those qualities needed to be a powerful part of God's kingdom and one day a part of a Godly marriage.

Pray that you and your future spouse grow closer to the Lord every day.
Pray that you both would seek God's wisdom when the road is unclear.
Pray both of you would seek God with a repentant heart when mistakes are made.
Pray that you and your future spouse keep your hearts in God's hands.

Yes, you marry one person, but more than likely, a family is attached to that person. I have witnessed the stress and struggles that plague a family resulting from relatives that don't support a family unit. These experiences showed me relatives do play a big part in forming a new family, and because of what I saw, I longed for a good relationship with my future in-laws. I don't know how or why I felt this so strongly, only that it must have been the Holy Spirit. I prayed specifically for years, that not only would God provide a wonderful husband, but that his family would love me for me and I could have a relationship with them.

As I began to get to know Kurtis' family, I quickly realized that if this was my future family, God had answered my prayers beyond what I could imagine. I still remember meeting some of his extended family around Christmastime and his aunt telling me that she daily prayed for us and some other young couples in her life. I was blown away. Here was this woman who had never met me, but regularly lifted us up before the Lord and cared about our spiritual well-being.

I know other family members prayed for us too, and it meant the world to me. I love his parents, and have enjoyed the fruits of those relationships. I have an absolute treasure in my sister-in-law and brother-in-law. They love Jesus with all the hearts and have the most caring and adventurous hearts of anyone I know. The Lord continued to answer my prayers in my brother's wife, who was my friend first before she and my brother started dating. To be friends first, then sisters for life, is an incredible blessing. What I tell people is that there is a lot of prayer behind the fruits of those relationships. It didn't just happen.

Writing Your Story

It's important to understand there is no magic formula for any relationship. Personalities, backgrounds, timing, life circumstances, families and so much more are vital factors in a dating relationship. For those of you who are in a more serious relationship, take some time to examine where you are. Are there some important conversations you've yet to have? Then talk about it. Are there some choices you need to make? Do it then, no hesitation. Are there some choices you need to quit making? Repent and make the changes, and keep moving forward.

I don't know what your situation is, but every relationship can benefit from honest prayer and reflection. Too often in our society, people flit about with a "Whatever" mentality...whatever happens, whatever I feel like, whatever I want, whatever you want. God calls his kids to more than just a "Whatever" mentality, especially when it comes to our relationships. I pray you have the courage to pursue God's best, and not use the world's best as a cop out.

CHAPTER FOUR
Change Your Expectations

You know the stories. The ones where husband and wife stand in front of their friends and family, each the only significant other they had ever had. They were each other's first sweetheart, their first kiss, and soon to be first intimate partner.

Somehow in Christian circles this is touted as not just a way to get married, but the elite way to get married. Sure, they talk about grace and how the Lord can be the Lord of all situations, but it's always made out to seem less than. There's a lot of pressure and pomp and circumstance to not give away your first kiss. Sounds like another area that the conversation needs to change.

The path to the marriage altar is not always straight or quick. We want it to be short and sweet with a Nashville filter. But that isn't usually the case, is it? The path is sometimes longer than we ever imagined. There are loops, backtracks, and bus stops we didn't anticipate. Is that any cause to worry and get discouraged? No way! The loops and twists in the path can teach us, helping us grow stronger in our relationship with Christ, while at the same time strengthening our relationship with others.

We saw this very same thing happen in our lives. Kurtis was not my first boyfriend. He was not the first boy I had given my emotions to. He was not the first guy I held hands with. He was not my first date. I was not Kurtis' first girlfriend, first kiss, or first love. Other people wrote on the pages of our hearts before our chapters brought us together. But what's more important is that we are each other's permanent love, and through it all, through all the unexpected detours in the path, we kept trusting God.

Zio's: The Place of First Dates

Confession: I had not one, not two, but three first dates at Zio's.

Zio's is an Italian restaurant in downtown Oklahoma City, and it hits a lot of right notes for a first date. More upscale than Fuzzy's or BWW, but not too high pressure like Melting Pot or a fancy steakhouse. Intimate without being intrusive. And the servers write their names for you upside down on the table, so that's something.

Anyway, my first date at Zio's came in between my freshman and sophomore years in college. I cleverly selected manicotti for my main dish, knowing I wouldn't have to tussle with pasta trailing out of my mouth. Yes, that was a real thought I had, as most girls have. Don't lie. You know you've thought it.

My date knew I liked photography, so he suggested we walk around the OKC Bombing Memorial after dinner so I could take pictures of the scenery. This would've gone great, except for the homeless guy who accosted us and asked for money, and then I proceeded to give more than my date to the homeless guy. I acted impulsively (blame it on my tender heart), and didn't really think how it might make him feel. My parents were horrified when I relayed the evening, and said I shouldn't have given more than my date did.

Well. That put a damper on my tender heart.

We went on another date to Pops, and my fun-loving self chose to order a Sprite. A SPRITE at Pops—home of like 12 million kinds of soda—and I pick THE MOST BORING ONE. That was the last date. He sporadically texted me in the months after, but I knew that chapter was closed.

It was probably the Sprite that did me in.

Round Two

Round Two came a year and a half later. This guy and I had been "talking" for about a month when we went on our first date, to Zio's of course. Home of first dates. We ate dinner, and went to see a movie afterward. Again, I ordered manicotti, seeing as I was such a woman of the world.

Then, during the movie, it happened. My date reached for my hand.

A guy who was not related to me or just standing next to me in a prayer circle had intentionally wanted to hold my hand. Maybe Zio's wasn't so bad after all. However, this relationship lasted only a few months, and I was relieved when it was over. It was not meant to be, and I was completely fine with that. God protected my emotions in that situation, and we parted ways.

Third Time (or Fettuccine) Was the Charm

Fast-forward five months and I find myself staring at a text from blind-date guy (now my husband) who suggested Zio's for our first date.

In true woman fashion, I agonized over my response for a solid thirty minutes.

Do I suggest some other place because I can't bear to visit Zio's a third time? Do I risk being perceived as picky? Also, all those servers at Zio's are sure to recognize me. (Right.) Or do I play it nice and flexible and say yes and risk my chances of a third first date at the same place? Also, maybe the manicotti was the problem? Yes, that had to be it. I could at least order something different.

Samantha, a woman of the world, clever beyond her years. Not.

As I usually default to being low maintenance, I said sure to Zio's and the rest is history.

I did order fettuccine alfredo that time, so you draw your own conclusions. Also, Kurtis recently remembered he had three first dates at Zio's as well, with me being the third. Again, draw your own conclusions.

Why do I say all this? Why does it even matter?

Because these three scenes represent a longer winding road that looked nothing like the dating gospel that had been presented to me. I battled at many points of wondering if I was making the right decisions. I battled my expectations not meeting reality. I struggled with people that seemed to fit perfectly in my life, but they melted into the background as quickly as they appeared. I struggled because all I wanted to know if I was doing a good job at this thing. I wanted to know if I was doing the *right* thing. This is really quite normal, but when you are in the midst of your own battles, it's hard to have that perspective.

Expectations

Why are our expectations so lofty? We want our romantic relationships to follow a linear course, like a love story in a movie that resolves in ninety minutes. It doesn't help that with the weaving of social media into our cultural fabric, we now know way more about other people's lives than what I believe we were ever intended to know. We know exactly how many of our friends are in relationships, engaged, or having babies. The running tallies are ever before us in Snaps and Clarendon or X-Pro II filters.

When milestones are popping up in everyone else's life, it's a constant reminder that they're not happening in yours. And it hurts. It hurts a lot. The best thing to do in regards to expectations is hold them lightly, not in death grip. Life is not passing by. You are not forgotten.

Trust that God's timing is preparing you perfectly and it hasn't "slipped His mind" to bring about someone to date, or to bring about a job, or whatever else you might be waiting on. Yes, life is a grand story, but it's not a movie. The plot of life won't resolve tightly just because you think it should.

Sometimes There's No Why

Besides my first boyfriend and the man I married, there were several other guys throughout college who either I was interested in, or they were interested in me. We'd start exchanging texts every so often, and then it was every day. I'd see them on campus more and more. Sometimes they would read more into my words and actions than what was actually there. Sometimes I would do the same. But then it would just…fizzle. The texts would slow, and then stop all together. Sometimes it happened abruptly. Personally, that was more hurtful than the one relationship that actually ended. There was a reason why my first boyfriend and I broke up, but I could never pinpoint the reason, the *why* of why these other relationships faded into the background. I want to know *why* so-and-so stopped talking to me, *why* he started hanging out with another girl, why I was suddenly not worth getting to know.

Rooted deep in my personality is a desire to assign meaning to the world around me, especially the struggles I go through. I want to trace the end results in a nice path back to the root of the problem. I want there to be a meaning to the struggles I've faced. The journalist in me desperately wants to know why. The writer in me wants there to be a story

There's a particular friendship of mine that has haunted my mind for years now, not because of what happened, but because of what *didn't* happen. Nothing happened, but there were (in my mind) several indications that the relationship could've gone farther. But it didn't.

I've tortured myself analyzing our interactions and conversations, trying to invent reasons and explanations of why nothing happened. In his mercy, the Lord gave me two thoughts for closure on this non-event. Isn't God gracious? He knows that sometimes we need closure, even when nothing has happened.

One was a tweet which, paraphrased, said that perhaps silence is all the closure you need. This freed me up so much to quit spending my mental energy trying to find the lock on a door that didn't even exist.

The other was a quote from Emily Freeman in *Simply Tuesday* which says, "Maybe there's no story at all. Perhaps it just is."[4]

Perhaps it just is. Let that settle into your soul for a moment.

On our path to the altar, we want each interaction, conversation, and relationship to be filled with meaning and weightiness. We want there to be a prince behind every frog, a hidden meaning in each rock. A story at every turn. But that is a fantasy.

Maybe you need to let a relationship, a friendship just be. It didn't move forward. It didn't blow up. There is no story to tell. It just is. And that is okay. Give yourself permission to let it be, and move on. Each interaction is shaping you. You wouldn't be who you are if it weren't for that. But don't let assigning meaning torture your soul. Sometimes, there is no why.

Sharing Our Story

Earlier, I talked about the loss of my grandpa right before I met Kurtis. A few weeks after Kurtis

---

[4] *Simply Tuesday.* Emily P. Freeman

and I officially started dating, a friend of mine was killed in a car accident. That was my first time to lose someone my own age, and it's a very different type of grief than losing someone who is older.

I remember feeling so vulnerable the week of her funeral, a turning point in coming to terms with my own fragility. At the time, I was not a crier (now I cry at almost every episode of *Fixer Upper*), but I cried, okay I sobbed, at this friend's funeral. This sudden exposure and vulnerability, the inescapable feeling of fragility, crashed in on me, and caused me to close up a part of my heart. I was devastated.

David Guetta's "Titanium" debuted in between my grandpa's death and meeting Kurtis. This song was everywhere that fall, playing over and over in my dance classes at college. Without realizing it, I think I wanted to be titanium to avoid any more hurt. So that's where I was emotionally and mentally. In case you're wondering, it did more harm than good. In ways, I think I'm still healing from that season emotionally. It's still hard for me to open up and I hate showing weaknesses. I hate unveiling vulnerabilities. But who does, really?

Anyway, back to the story. Our relationship was progressing fine throughout the fall and winter (or so I thought), but Kurtis remained unsure if I liked "liked" him. I was reticent with my compliments and emotions. Even though we were cautious about hugs and such, I withheld from any minor flirtatious prodding or encouragement. Along with my perfectionist tendencies of not wanting to say or do the wrong thing in a relationship, I see how I must have been a tough nut to crack. What a mess was I. He was prepared to break up with me because he just wasn't sure where I stood, and I a) didn't realize he thought these things and b) was stressed and scared with how I needed to move forward.

It came to a head the week of our first Valentine's Day celebration when I had to tell Kurtis we couldn't have dinner at his house, per my parents' rule. I was so embarrassed, and although he acquiesced, I knew he was frustrated. I thought he would be done with me at that time, but we made other plans for later in the week. On our date, I finally opened up about my feelings. The timing couldn't have been riper. We said the words we had been wanting to say for a while, but just didn't know how. And we shared our first kiss.

It was a curvy path, but we got there. God moved on our behalf, in spite of ourselves. Thank goodness for that power.

Embrace Each Phase

I learned such important lessons in each phase of our relationship: from just getting to know each other, to falling in love, to being engaged. I needed the time in each phase to get reacquainted with myself. In the beginning of our relationship, I had not yet experienced being in a relationship with someone of that stability and consistency. That was new. I was learning to trust another human in a new way, learning to open myself up.

When we both expressed we wanted to get married, but weren't engaged yet, that was an important time as well. I had never been in love before, and all of those feelings and emotions were brand new. I relished them. I needed those four months from the time we said "I love you" until the time Kurtis asked me to marry him.

When we did get engaged, that was another important training ground as the next checkpoint before marriage. I learned a lot more about our roles in the marriage, sex, and handling conflict in the five months of our engagement.

Each phase of a relationship has value. Learn from each phase, don't feel pressure to rush it. Some move quickly from dating to engagement. For others, there is a long period of dating or a long period of engagement. Whatever your situation calls for, don't get stuck in the comparison trap. Live in your own story, and embrace each phase of your relationship.

CHAPTER FIVE

Change the Atmosphere

Let's talk about sex now.
How's that for a transition? Sex is after all, the reason I'm even here writing this book, and the reason you are sitting there reading it. Two people had sex and created me. The same can be said for why you are here. See, do you feel guilty just reading those sentences? Why?

By a show of hands, who thought that sex was bad while growing up? Me too. It's not that my parents ever said, "Sex is bad," but I never got the impression that it was good, either. Don't talk about it, don't ask about it, and whatever you do, don't do IT. Until you're married of course. One day it's bad. The next day, good. Huh?

Stay with me. I promise I'm going somewhere with this.

Desires by Design

God created sex to unite two people and forge their spirits together in untold ways. Sex, and sexual desires are good and right, within marriage. God designed sex after all. He's not surprised it's enjoyable or pleasurable. He is not embarrassed by that fact that his children enjoy intimacy. In regard to these sexual desires, God did not design our desires to slow down. When you are with the person you love, it's normal and right to feel excited and bubbly on the inside. It is right to want to be close to them and desire their presence.

However, this part of "the talk" is usually cut out, and it jumps straight into boundaries, and how powerful our sexual desires are, and how bad it is to get pregnant out of wedlock. Too often, kids walk away from "the talk" with the impression that sex is more ugly than beautiful, more scary than powerful. Okay, it does seem a little scary no matter what, but hopefully you catch my drift. After years of these type of conversations in the home and church, when young adults do finally arrive at the altar, and head into marriage, sex can sometimes still feel wrong. It still feels off-limits. A necessity, but too taboo to discuss any further. Dear friends, the conversation *cannot* end there. It has to keep going to show that God has beautiful, powerful vision for sexual intimacy in marriage.

Parents, whether you realize it or not, more and more Christian millennials are voicing their feelings of guilt or shame over enjoying sex *inside* marriage.

In a 2015 *Relevant* magazine article, writer Lily Dunn echoes this sentiment:

> *"While we intellectually believed that sex was a good thing that was intended for enjoyment in marriage, we had spent years conditioning ourselves to respond to sexual feelings with fear, guilt and shame. In the space of a few hours, something we had treated as forbidden, dangerous and private became something we*

> *were meant to enjoy and celebrate with each other. No amount of intellectual knowledge could take those deeply ingrained feelings towards our sexuality and magically change them the moment we slipped on those rings or later when we slipped off our wedding clothes."*[5]

It's not that it's impossible to mentally separate that sex is only okay in marriage, but subconsciously, this message leaves little triggers of guilt and shame that can take months, if not years to disarm. God designed sex to be beautiful and powerful, within a certain context. While the message of a "certain context" was emphasized, the beauty and power was minimized in books I read growing up, scattered messages from the church, and even more scant conversations with the adults in my life.

If you find this surprising as parents, it may be that your children never felt like they could bring up such topics when they were younger, and thus

---

[5] http://www.relevantmagazine.com/life/relationships/how-im-overcoming-guilt-my-sex-life

never voiced concerns and questions as they got older. An atmosphere of discussion had never been created, and by then, it's too late.

An August 2015 Barna study sought to explore the attitudes and mindsets toward sex across the generations. Roxanne Stone, editor-in-chief of the Barna group, spoke to the diverse findings.

> "The big story here is how little everyone agrees on when it comes to the purpose of sex, says Stone. Whereas practicing Christians still overwhelmingly tie sex to marriage, the move among the greater U.S. population—most evidently among younger generations—is a de-linking of marriage and sex. Sex has become less a function of procreation or an expression of intimacy and more of a personal experience. To have sex is increasingly seen as a pleasurable

> *and important element in the journey toward self-fulfillment."*[6]

This to me is a rally cry for new life to be injected into the vision of marriage. And it starts with cultivating an atmosphere of discussion in the home, to be later (hopefully) supported by the church.

Atmosphere of Discussion

I've thought a lot about this in the time since Kurtis and I have been married, and wondered how I would address this topic with my future children. Will I feel differently once I have kids? Will it be harder to be open and forthcoming? Honestly, I can't answer that question, since I'm not there yet. But I do know what it's like to be in the kid's position. I don't think as Christians that we can in good conscience continue to perpetuate this cycle of silencing sex. Could that maybe be the root of a lot of problems? How can problems be fixed, how can they be addressed if no one says anything?

Blogger Melissa Edgington puts it this way:

---

[6] https://www.barna.org/research/culture-media/research-release/what-americans-believe-about-sex

> "As Christian parents, we want to disciple our kids and lead them in the ways of God. We can't fool ourselves into thinking that sex education isn't a huge part of discipleship...sex shouldn't be a dirty word in Christian homes. If we want our kids to think biblically about sex and about their own worth, then we have to teach them what the Bible says about it, one conversation at a time."[7]

Yes, discussing sex can usher in painful baggage and past trauma. There is also a line to walk of introducing too much too soon. While I can't answer the question of what is right for your family, I do know that the conversations should start small and be approached with love and discretion. Waiting a week before the wedding to broach the topic is too late. Waiting until college to talk about it is too late. High school may be too late.

Not sure where to start? Ask the kids if they have questions. Ask what they've heard their

---

[7] http://yourmomhasablog.com/2016/02/16/sex-education-should-start-in-the-christian-home/

friends talk about it. Walk them through scripture and point to what God says. Always point to what God says. Give them small portions of books to read, and then have a discussion. Listen to a podcast or watch a video on YouTube of a sermon or a pastor teaching on marriage and intimacy, and see what conversations arise from that. Maybe parents, this really is a topic too toxic for you to broach with your kids. Help your kids find a trusted adult who can be that open line of communication.

Addressing Pornography

The other reason to foster an environment in which kids feel like they can share and ask questions is to head off deep-rooted problems, like pornography.

I've listened to teens *in the church* share about struggles and addiction with pornography. Parents, you can't wait until your kid has questions. You can't wait for them to find pornography; pornography is already finding them.

Start conversations with your kids now, as awkward as it may be. Because someone is having the conversation with your kids, whether you like it or not, whether you know it or not. They may not even realize what it is, or how harmful it can be. According to another recent Barna study on pornography, teens aren't even ranking pornography very high on the moral indiscretion scale.

> "When asked to rank a series of "bad things" a person could do—things such as stealing, lying, having an affair, even overeating—teens and young adults placed all porn-related actions at the very bottom of the list. In fact, teens and young adults said "Not Recycling" is more immoral than viewing pornographic images. They also placed "thinking negatively about someone with a different point of view" as a much worse activity than viewing pornography."[8]

Again, the conversation needs to change, as evidenced by these attitudes toward this sin. Pornography doesn't just affect one person, but the

---

[8] https://www.barna.org/blog/culture-media/roxanne-stone/the-sexting-crisis

whole community. It doesn't matter if it' a "spam" account or a girlfriend/boyfriend sexting, pornography has massive collateral damage.

Will this be an easy topic to broach? Hardly. But you are the adult in the situation, you are the parent, the adult that cares most about them in this whole world. As the parent, you have the prime position to guide and influence and inform and protect. Your kids need to hear your instruction, as well as learn from your mistakes.

Students and young adults, if this is already an area of temptation and struggle for you, speak up. Yes, it's painful. But now is the time to deal with this sin. I may not know your particular situation, but I'm willing to bet there are caring adults in your life who can help bring whatever struggles and addictions to the light and help you deal with it how Jesus wants us to deal with it.

To expect future romantic relationships to flourish in spite of hidden sexual sin is the biggest lie ever. Hiding these addictions and struggles is like carrying a ticking time bomb, ignoring the fact that it could go off at any moment. The bomb can go off at any time, causing major damage to a promising relationship, or even a marriage. And there are no guarantees on how much will be repaired. Get help now. Do it for yourself. Do it for your future spouse. Do it because God calls Christians to something far more beautiful and powerful than lusting after Photoshopped images on a screen and a temporary high.

Vision for the Future

The desire of my heart is to cultivate an environment in which any future children of mine feel comfortable addressing a topic that is close to God's heart. It should still be approached with discretion and honor, but if kids don't feel like they can talk to their own parents about these issues, we already know where they'll get their info from: other ill-informed children or the sex-crazed culture we live in.

Going back to the Foundation chapter, if Christian families don't lay a foundation of sex-education that begins with Christ, it's planning for failure. If kids don't see early on that Christ created our bodies, created sex, created these desires, they won't know where it all fits in a confusing world. If they don't see early on that it's Christ who determines their worth, not how many sexual conquests they make, or how certain body parts look, then what message are we sending them? If they don't know they were created for a higher purpose than to sext and sleep around, why are we surprised at pornography addictions, teen pregnancies, STDs?

Christ has to be the foundation for every aspect of our walk with Christ, and that includes our mentality towards dating, marriage, and sex.

Sharing Our Story

The best way I can describe my knowledge of sex and the role of sex in marriage before our wedding day is a blank canvas. I had no vision and little understanding, good or bad. In a way, this was a blessing. Two books Kurtis and I read before we got married laid the majority of my foundation and understanding of sex within a Christian marriage: *Love and Respect* and *The Language of Sex*. The Holy Spirit guided my heart and mind as we read through these books, and for the first time, I saw God's vision for sex inside marriage. I saw His heart in creating something so powerful that draws two people together in untold ways. Ways that were noble and special, not shameful.

Kurtis and I had a handful of meaningful conversations *before* we got married about sex. Not fantasies, but honest talks about expectations, practical issues, and fears we had. One of the most helpful things Kurtis said was that he didn't have expectations, and that part of the fun was learning together. This lifted a burden off my mind that I didn't even know was there.

When the wedding night came, no tension was threaded through the atmosphere, but joy. It took courage to have those conversations with each other beforehand, but if we didn't, I believe it would've severely stunted our intimacy.

A Final Word on Purity

As children of God, those who have accepted Christ's payment on their behalf for sins, we are made pure. Our very nature has been changed to pure and holy, otherwise, God couldn't have a relationship with us. Yes, we still mess up, but that doesn't change our standing before God. Yes, we may still have consequences to deal with, but as children of God, we are still pure and holy before him. Sex before marriage does not make you impure, and neither does abstaining from sex make you "more" pure. That still puts the focus on works to make us pure or not. We are only made pure by the work of the Holy Spirit in our hearts.

King David in the Old Testament committed adultery and was accessory to a murder. His world came crashing down when his guard was down. When God looked in David's heart, he saw a need for repentance, but he still saw "a man after His own heart." God in His love and mercy sent a messenger to convict David, not condemn him. David was broken, and repented. His story is a pattern and encouragement for us. When we do mess up, look for where God is bringing conviction and respond.

> *"Create in me a pure heart, O God, and renew a steadfast spirit within me. Do not cast me from your presence or take your Holy Spirit from me. Restore to me the joy of your salvation and grant me a*

willing spirit, to sustain me." Psalm 51:10-12 9 (NIV)

Note: Guys, feel free to skip to the next chapter, "In the Meantime (Guys)"

PART THREE

CHAPTER SIX

In the Meantime: For Ladies

> *"Don't let anyone look down on you because you are young, but set an example for the believers in speech, in conduct, in love, in faith and in purity."* 1 Timothy 4:12 (NIV)

In my fourth grade art class, the girls sat on the left side of the room, the boys on the right, and never did the two sides mix. The classroom is as vivid in my mind today as if I had just been there. In elementary school, girls and boys seem to naturally separate. Even though I had a brother and got along great with him, it was the understood rule that boys were weird, rude, and gross. Girls rule, boys drool as the playground war cry goes. The marriage altar is a practically non-existent dot on the horizon in fourth grade art class.

But at some point (ahem, puberty), the game changes. Or rather, the game starts.

Boys are not icky now. Now we want to talk to them, but sometimes they don't want to talk to us. We want to know if they notice us, like us. We still want certain boys to stay away, but want other ones to come closer. But come closer to us, not our friends.

At this point in my life, I have still spent more time being single than I have been in a relationship or been married. I'm imagining it's the same for you. That means there is a lot of time to spend well "in the meantime."

What do you do in the meantime? In my opinion, the culture and even the Church can put so much emphasis on *finding* the right person, that sometimes we forget that *we* have to *be* the right person for someone else. Now is the time to build the character and perseverance that is needed to be united in marriage and nurture a family. Now is the time to invest in relationships like your family and close friends. Now is the time to explore your passions and ministry opportunities. That all sounds great on paper, but what does that really look like in real life? It all starts right now with the family you are already a part of.

Pillars in a Palace

> *"Then our sons in their youth will be like well-nurtured plants, and our daughters will be like pillars carved to adorn a palace."* Psalm 144:12 (NIV)

I love these words from Psalm 144. As daughters in training to be wives and mothers, this Psalm speaks to our importance in the family structure.

"Our daughters like carved pillars, cut for the structure of a palace."

This speaks of an emotional, mental, spiritual strength needed to support a home and not give way beneath increased weight of responsibility, setbacks, and day-to-day drudgery. God designed daughters to unite a family, just like columns bring a building together. God designed daughters to beautify a home, just like columns add grace and beauty to any structure. What a noble calling.

As you read through this section, ask yourself: *do I make my family more or less sturdy?* During this time before you are in a dating relationship, there's no better time to work on being God's pillar in your family. A daughter's role will look a little different in every family, depending on personality and circumstances. There's not one right way to be "God's column" but typically, columns support, unite, and adorn whatever structures they are a part of. How can you apply that in your own life?

Support

Daughters can provide meaningful emotional and spiritual support to their families and close friends. As we grow and learn in the Lord, we learn how to use our emotional sensitivities for good and not for drama. When you feel a wave of drama rising up in you, look instead for opportunities to listen, to use empathy to put yourself in other's shoes, and provide encouragement where needed. That takes the focus off of you for a moment, and on to others, giving you some time to collect your thoughts. This is also a great time to practice sharing your heart in this safe environment, whether addressing conflict or expressing frustration.

Because I loathe conflict, I struggled expressing myself in hurt and frustration at home and in our dating relationship. I still have to work on it in our marriage. I learned that Kurtis was actually more hurt when I held back in moments of hurt, anger, or irritation. I assumed he would be irritated with my moments of irritation and I just wanted to skip that scene altogether. However, I learned (and am still learning) that guys in general don't like situations where they feel like they can't win. To clearly state messages of "I am angry and here's why" was far better than to leave him guessing, or leave him out of the solution because I didn't want to be a bother. It takes courage to state what's bothering you, but it is better to get it out in the open if it's really something worth discussing.

The years I lived at home also gave me great time to practice listening. My brother loved to talk with me at night, sharing whatever was on his heart. He didn't really need my advice; he just wanted a listening, supportive ear. My husband today needs those same things. By investing in that relationship with my brother, we grew stronger together, but it also prepared me for marriage.

Over the years, I also had many opportunities to encourage my dad through notes and through prayers, something I do for my husband today. I loved hiding notes in my dad's suitcase when he went on a business trip, or putting notes in his car before work. The small things you do for your family today do have an impact on tomorrow. Be encouraged that it is worthwhile, not a waste of time.

In order to offer this kind of support, you need to still dig down deep into your foundation of Christ. It's a relationship you will never stop building, but take advantage of this time when you are the least distracted. Spending time with Christ reveals who you are in him and strengthens you, enabling you to practice giving emotional and spiritual support to the people you call family. Even if you have a tough family situation in which you feel completely helpless, and unable to affect the outcome, don't give up. Continue to be faithful in the small ways of providing support where you can to your family.

Unite

Not only do daughters provide emotional and spiritual support to their families, but they also have the power to unite their family. Uniting any family, team, or organization happens through words and actions. Do you unite your family with your words and actions? Or do you divide your family members, playing one off the other in an attempt to get your own way? Do you seek to play one parent off the other? Do you cause so much strife that it puts stress on your relationships with your siblings and parents?

Like I said earlier, columns were designed to provide greater strength to a structure, not make it weaker. Ask the Lord to help you set aside your flesh, and instead use your words and actions to unite your family.

Adorn

Your inner life brings grace to the family. Remember, it's not about being perfect, but about letting Jesus shine through you. You elevate and lift your family not through your outward appearance, but through your heart. Do you look for ways you can add to the family, or do you focus on how the family meets your needs? You have the power to beautify your family and elevate them through your graceful inner life. One day, that character will grace your husband.

> *"A wife of noble character is her husband's crown, but a disgraceful wife is like decay in his bones."*
> *Proverbs 12:4 (NIV)*

Don't discount those opportunities by thinking this season of your life doesn't really matter. You have an important role to play now *right now*. You have a necessary and irreplaceable part in your story. Your story doesn't start when you date someone or when you get married. It doesn't stop there either. You are living your story now.

"That our daughters may be as cornerstones... I think one may read the love and tenderness of the Lord in this apparently casual but intended expression, and that he meant the nations of the earth to know and understand how much of their happiness, their strength, and their security was dependent on the female children of a family." —Barton Bouchier[9]

Investing Your Time Well

> *"Teach us to number our days, that we may gain a heart of wisdom."*
> *Psalm 90:12 (NIV)*

Lastly, I want to address your most important resource: time. Your time is one of your most valuable resources. How are you spending it? Who are you spending it on? Throughout high school and early on in college, I was focused on my

---

[9] *The Treasury of David.* Charles Spurgeon

education and dance training. Because of my energy and time spent on those pursuits, I was able to earn scholarships that paid for nearly all of my college education, and also provided a source of income through teaching dance. All those years I spent going to classes, rehearsals, and competitions gave me the experience I needed to lead a class on my own. All the time I spent doing homework and pushing myself earned me scholarships so I didn't have to worry about money throughout college. That was time well spent. The same can be said for whatever job or career you find yourself in. During this same time, I explored worship arts ministry and children's ministry. I learned how I can contribute to the body of Christ in these areas and discovered how much I love teaching.

You never know what the next days are going to hold, but investing time in your education and ministry pursuits will always reap a harvest. Investing too early or too often in romantic relationships does not always guarantee the same return. Use your time wisely. You can't get it back once it's spent.

CHAPTER SEVEN

In the Meantime: For Guys

Since this chapter is speaking more directly to the guys, I thought it best to let Kurtis take over and share his thoughts. Girls, feel free to skip on to the next chapter.

***

While there are many of the same things as girls that guys need to focus on "in the meantime," there are a few specific things I want to address to the guys.

Access

As men, being visual means we're easily swayed. God created us that way, but that can't become a default excuse. What is a practical way to keep our eyes and hearts from wandering down paths we shouldn't? Guard the access to tempting situations, which mainly means, lock down all sources to the Internet. Locking devices down and having accountability partners are the only way to combat the temptations out there. We all think we can do it on our own, but the reality is no one is strong enough alone. Lock down access to temptations, whatever that might be for you, and let God be in the driver's seat. Sexual temptation is one in which God instructs us to flee from, to run away from. (1 Corinthians 6:18) Not flirt with. Not test ourselves, but run far and fast away from it. We don't have strength in ourselves to fight temptation, but he has all the strength we'll ever need to fight whatever temptation comes across our path.

> *"Look to the Lord and his strength; seek his face always."* Psalm 105:4 (NIV)

I put this first because that's the first step. Without this step, you can look good externally, but internally, you could be moments away from hitting rock bottom. Marriages are broken because of sexual immorality and addictions. Other relationships are damaged because of sexual addictions. Trust in relationships is a precious commodity, and secrets like pornography addictions, affairs, are capable of completely destroying that trust. If you do not get control of it as a teenager, it's unlikely you'll get control of it as an adult. In a 2016 Barna study on porn, called "The Porn Phenomenon," the stats are sickening.

> *"Among teen and young adult men, 81 percent ever seek it out and 67 percent at least monthly. Among men ages 25-plus, the comps are 65 percent and 47 percent...62 percent of teens and young adults have received a sexually explicit image and 41 percent have*

> sent one (usually from/to their boy/girlfriend or friend)."[10]

The reality is the longer you let your flesh rule, the harder it is to overcome. But God doesn't leave us in a lurch. He made us. He knows our hearts and, he desires that we come to him with all of our burdens, including sexual temptation. His given us his Holy Spirit, and his given us a gift in our fellow brothers in Christ. There is built-in accountability in our youth groups, small groups, and church leadership. Will it be easy to open those lines of communication and submit to accountability? No. Like Samantha said earlier in the book, sometimes these conversations are awkward, but the results are life-giving. Yes, it's so hard to have the conversation, but once it starts, it's gold. Once it starts it creates a bond that is motivation to not settle for the trash the world floats around us, but to keep our eyes on God's best.

Again, access is the first step. Don't fall in the trap of thinking you're invincible, only to hurt

---

[10] https://www.barna.org/blog/culture-media/david-kinnaman/the-porn-phenomenon#.Vzs0shUrLBJ

others that you had no intention of hurting, in addition to damaging your own heart and mind. The reality is: porn isn't just about you. It's not just about you getting aroused, feeling good about yourself, or feeling like a man. That's a lie. Whether it be a parent, a friend you cause to stumble, or your spouse or girlfriend learning about your addiction, it hurts others more than you can fathom. It creates wounds that while they may heal, there will always be scars. Trust that is broken that is never truly the same. This is a battle for your life, for your heart, so treat it as one.

Ask the Right Questions

"So where did you guys meet?"

This is a question any married couple will tell you they get regularly. So many adults are secretive about this. I wonder why? Could it be because they're embarrassed by the decisions they made in the past? Possibly. I would encourage you to look at the atmosphere in which you are looking for a girl. Is it a bar? College parties? Other kinds of parties? Work? Church? There is not one formula for where to meet a good woman. In fact, I'm sure many men may have met their wife at a bar, and then took her to church and it all worked out. But more often than not, those guys who have met women at the bar found themselves in rocky situations soon afterward. If you build your foundation on rocky circumstances, your future relationship will be on rocky ground. It won't magically change. So what atmosphere are you looking for a woman in?

> *"Do not be yoked together with unbelievers. For what do righteousness and wickedness have in common? Or what fellowship can light have with darkness?" 2 Corinthians 6:14 (NIV)*

Now, obviously relationships don't just start at bars or church. Maybe you're not old enough for a bar and met at a high school party. So, let's back up: where you meet the girl will tell you something about her. But where you meet the girl won't tell you *all* you need to know. Where you meet her also won't tell you the condition of her heart. Just because she goes to church doesn't mean her heart is captured by God. Has she just gone to church all her life because her parents wanted her to, or because her friends are there?

When Samantha and I met, we met at a coffee shop. This was probably horribly misleading to her because I don't do coffee, or frappa-whatevers. But while it was my first time to even meet her, I could immediately tell she was thoughtful. I immediately knew she loved God. Not the shallow type of love, but the deep, longing for a relationship with God type of love. I immediately knew she had plans for her future. You know why I knew these things? I was asking questions. Sure, I didn't learn all I needed to know, but from date one to two to three to four, I confirmed every step of the way she was type of woman I was searching for, and the type of woman would help me grow and cultivate a deeper relationship with God. We need to ask the right questions, and make an effort to look beyond just a pretty face and an easy laugh.

Is she a Christian?

Did you ask? Because if you didn't, don't assume. But don't stop there. Keep the conversation going.

What's her favorite Bible verse?

What's her favorite book of the Bible?

What has God shown her lately?

These answers will tell you her heart. And be prepared with your own answers, because she will more than likely turn that question back on you.

What is her background?

When did she become a Christian?

What's her family life like?

If you don't have much in common with your backgrounds, it's better to know that upfront. All these questions and decisions lead to this: *does she have a faith that will last*? Life is long. To build a marriage that lasts, you need to make sure she's someone who will help you grow. Someone who will support your goals. As guys, we're pretty confident. But nothing will break your confidence more than when your woman doesn't support you. If her foundation in Christ is good, you can put down strong roots that will support a lifetime of dreams, hopes, and endeavors for the kingdom of God.

This list is not a full list of questions to ask in a relationship by any means. I'd challenge you to find an even bigger list, and make it a point to discuss every question on that list in a dating relationship. Maybe not all at once, your girl might freak out on you.

Remember: dating ultimately should lead to marriage. Dating just to date is an empty pursuit, like chasing wind.

What it Means to Lead

When Samantha and I were dating, I had to explore what it meant to lead in a dating relationship. Leading sounds simple, but what does it mean in action? I was extremely fortunate because Samantha was very willing to be led. But leading for me in our relationship meant consciously asking questions. Leading meant setting boundaries (and talking about them) immediately. All it takes is a little bit of courage. Now let's dive in.

Habits can take a while to build, right? Habits like doing your homework on time, putting away laundry, getting a quiet time in or exercising regularly. But by working on those habits, they become ingrained in us. They become a part of us. So whether you are dating someone or not, there are things you can practice to become intentional leaders. Being a man doesn't just happen. You have to be a man on purpose.

First, make the effort to lead now. Not tomorrow, not next year, not when you are a junior or senior. If you don't lead now, it will be harder and harder to lead in the future. What does it mean to lead in a dating relationship? I'm so glad you asked. Taking the lead doesn't mean bossing your woman around. To lead means protecting her, cherishing her and making the tough decisions (regarding boundaries, reading the Bible, going to church) without her prodding.

A good leader sets the tone with intentional conversations and activities. I promise you, your girl will be impressed.

Maybe you are catching the vision for all of this. Or maybe this all seems like a lot work, or completely foreign to you. Maybe you haven't seen this modeled in your own life because your dad wasn't around, your older brothers made poor decisions, or there just aren't a lot of guys around. I would encourage you to find a guy that can be that mentor in your life. Someone older, wiser, and loves Jesus. That's another step to being a good leader: knowing when to get help.

Second, being a leader in a relationship also means having a clear direction. What are the goals you have in life? What are the goals you have for your relationship? Career goals, family goals, "dreaming big" shows a girl you have a purpose. These goals should be fleshed out through prayer and discussion with a mentor, like we just talked about. Catch that? A mentor, not your best friend. A mentor offers wisdom our friends can't, because they have already been down that road. They've made a few mistakes, and by listening to them, you can avoid some biggies. Maybe there's a mentor in your life that already has a family, or has been married for a while. Ask them what it's like to be a husband, to lead a family, to hold down a job, etc. They can help you flesh out goals for your own life.

"Where there is no vision, the people perish..." Proverbs 29:18a (KJV)

Setting the tone and asking questions was hit upon in the last section, but I want to reiterate: you have to ask the questions. If you're being the leader and have a direction in life, you need to ask questions that can confirm your dating partner is on the same page. Many promising relationships have ended after years because the partners had different plans for their life. Not even bad plans, just different.

For example, one partner might have always had a dream of being a foreign missionary. After years of dating, this partner wanted to make it happen, but the significant other wasn't on the same page. They had to part ways, but it could have happened so much sooner if they'd had the right conversations. Other conflicting desires might arise in where you choose to live, go to college, or your home church.

One example of these conversations early in my relationship with Samantha was homeschooling. Samantha had been homeschooled 1st-12th grade, while I had attended public school my whole life. Our school experiences were very different, and while I was familiar with homeschooling, I didn't know exactly what it meant. Even before our first date, the girl who set us up told me "she was homeschooled." All the homeschooling stereotypes ran through my head, unfortunately. But on that first date I *asked*. We had extended discussions about what it meant to her and her family, why she wanted to homeschool her kids in the future, and how she wanted to do it. Over the course of the following months, I began to see that homeschooling fit in with my own vision for my future family. Before we got engaged, I knew I too wanted to homeschool my kids. Is that a relationship make-it-or-break-it moment? No, but it is a big deal. By having the conversation early and listening, we were able to come to an agreement before it ever become an issue.

Third, if your girlfriend is not a Christian, seriously evaluate your motives for being in the relationship in the first place. Think back the Foundations chapter. If you are a Christian, but your girlfriend isn't, it's like building a house on an uneven or broken foundation. There are problems from the outset. You two will never see eye-to-eye because you have different motivations and priorities in life. Sure, it's fine to be friends with non-Christians; God even calls us to that. But if you cannot pray with your girlfriend, if you all can't talk about God, if she has no interest in going to church, serving, or learning about God, she won't be someone who will help you have a closer relationship with God. It may be time to part ways.

With each answer or discussion, you need to evaluate: are we on the same page? If you are, great. If not? Well, that's for you to decide.

A Call to Man Up

> *"May our sons in their youth be like plants full grown." Psalm 144:12 (NIV)*

I loved how Samantha used the other part of this verse in the "For Ladies' Only" chapter. Guys, now it's our turn. To me, this image speaks of building maturity, strength, and responsibility, even before the world expects it. Remember, as young men of God we are called to a different standard. There's no time to wait for people to hand us things, to act like victims, or waste time in front of the TV. While many guys around you may be content to hang out in a "delayed adolescence," you can make a different choice. You can choose to lock down access to temptation and not let it control you. You can choose to surround yourself with positive mentors who help you shape your goals for your walk with God, education, career and family. You can choose to ask meaningful questions, versus continuously engage in mindless chatter.

Dating in light of the cross isn't just "fun," it goes beyond that. Dating with the goal of marriage seeks to join up two followers of God. That's serious business. Take it seriously and only date women you would honestly want to marry. Anything short of this leads to relationship mistakes and bad marriages that may or may not be able to be repaired. In the end, if you don't respect and love her enough to marry her, you're less likely to respect the boundaries of a dating relationship and could end up in a bedroom together.

If you limit your access, ask the right questions, and seek to be an intentional leader, then you are on the right road, regardless if you are dating yet or not. As a man of God, that means taking responsibility for your actions, for your life. The words from Proverbs 20 are haunting:

> *"Most men will proclaim every one his own goodness: but a faithful man who can find?"* Proverbs 20:6 (KJV)

Have you been "proclaiming your own goodness," thinking you have it all together and can sweep any girl off her feet? In our own strength, this isn't possible. In our own strength, we can't be faithful. Let this be a challenge to look to God's strength continually to become the men of God he's called us to be. Regardless if there is a woman or not by your side.

AFTERWORD

Yeah, But Waiting Still Sucks

I hear you. I get it. If you just read through this section and thought *Yeah, well, I've done all that and waiting still sucks,* be encouraged that you *are* on the right track. For the ladies, you are providing emotional and spiritual support to your family (or those you consider family), you are investing in your relationship with Christ, and you are making the most of education and other talents. You are being a good steward of what God has given you.

Guys, I can see you are working hard to guard your eyes and heart, you are working to set goals for yourself, and are training to be leaders.

I won't try to tell you that it's not discouraging or disappointing when friends around you are dating, getting engaged, and getting married. I would not dare to cheapen these feelings. But just remember, life is not a race, and you are not less because something isn't happening for you.

As I write this book, I'm waiting for something as well. My husband and I have been trying to start a family for two years, and it just hasn't happened yet, but it's happened for many of our friends around us. Those familiar specters of disappointment, hurt, and jealousy still haunt our minds and hearts. I've screamed at God more than once, asking why someone else gets to start a family and we don't. We've followed the Lord's path. We are responsible adults. It feels like we've held up our end of the bargain, and God hasn't followed through on His.

My point in sharing this is that these same struggles can attack us at any point in our journey. You think your life would finally be in sync if God would just do (fill in the blank). I'm here to say that you won't last long with that mentality. Our strength is depleted when we are waiting on an event. I can't explain why we haven't had a baby yet. I can't explain why you don't have a boyfriend or girlfriend yet. But I do know that God is faithful, and it's just like the enemy to get us to feel "less." Keep your eyes on the Lord, and keep His faithful nature ever present in your mind, for *"those who seek the* L<small>ORD</small> *lack no good thing."* (Psalm 34:10b) And remember that no matter where you are in life, whether you feel like you have been waiting a long time for something to happen, you are not less.

CONCLUSION

After the Honeymoon

Throughout high school, I can think of three specific instances when God used different people to encourage me on the path I was on in praying for a husband. These talks came at just the right time, and I took them as pep talks straight from heaven. Each conversation confirmed that God was able to bring the right person into my life at the right time. Each time, I was encouraged that God did see me, and knew where my heart was. Each time I was motivated to keep going. One speaker honestly stated that it only gets harder from this point on to keep your eyes on Jesus with the pulls and temptations in dating. She was right; and I was fed by her honesty.

I don't know where this book finds you; maybe you're in high school, maybe you're in college, maybe you're done with college. Hopefully something tugs at your heart from this book. Hopefully God speaks to you through these pages like he spoke to me through certain people. Hopefully you'll see in your own life where you need to check your foundation and see if it's built on Jesus. You'll hopefully check your definition of purity. And hopefully, you'll be encouraged to change the conversation in regards to the intentions, expectations and atmosphere of Christian dating, and to also live your "meantime" at full throttle.

With several years between me and "where is my husband?" prayers, I've gained a little perspective. Namely, God knows what he is doing. His timing was perfect. The young men which he turned away from my path would not have been a good fit. I would not have been a good fit for them. It's so hard to accept this *in the midst of*: the midst of waiting, the midst of no "special person" in sight. But God has all of his children in his sights, as well as you in his sights. He has not forgotten. He has not overlooked. Be encouraged that God can see over the mountain, and knows how to bring his children together.

He created marriage, remember? He performed the first wedding ceremony. He is the ultimate matchmaker.

In our few years since saying "I Do," we've seen that purity doesn't stop at the marriage altar. In some ways, a new chapter in purity is just beginning. Marriage is not the time to relax on building character and pursuing God's best. Now is the time to see fruit, and it's also the time to start planting a new harvest. Marriage will reveal far more in your life and in the life of your spouse that needs the loving touch of Christ than you thought possible.

Marriage also doesn't mean the end of fun and wonder. Our culture would like you to believe the fun ends on the flight home from the honeymoon. It's a choice we refuse to make. It's not all perfect, but marriage certainly isn't boring.

CHANGE THE CONVERSATION

Our story is still being written, as is yours. We pray that you take you great delight in the Lord, as he delights in you. We pray that you find the courage and joy in building authentic community around you. We pray that you learn from your mistakes, and then move on. We pray that you would find the courage to have those tough conversations and be your truest self, because our true selves are irresistible and lovely. And we pray that you will always be ready for how the Lord may decide to move in your life.

Because hey, you might meet your spouse on your next trip to Starbucks.

Love,
The Hannis

Thanks for sticking with me and finishing the book!
I'd love to connect with you.
Check out my blog, **A Word in Season** at **mrshanni.com** and sign up for my newsletter today and receive some freebies!

Coming Christmas 2016...

BLOOM

FRESH DEVOTIONS FOR GIRLS

Made in the USA
Charleston, SC
09 June 2016